WRITTEN COMMUNICATION

Gail B. Stewart

BLACKBIRCH®
PRESS

THOMSON

GALE

San Diego • Detroit • New York • San Francisco • Cleveland • New Haven, Conn. • Waterville, Maine • London • Munich

For more information, contact
The Gale Group, Inc.
27500 Drake Rd.
Farmington Hills, MI 48331-3535
Or you can visit our Internet site at http://www.gale.com

Picture Credits

Cover: © Art Today, Inc. (both)
© Art Today, Inc., 5 (right), 7, 31
© Bettmann/CORBIS, 9, 16, 25, 26, 27 (both), 28 (top)
© COREL Corporation, 5 (inset), 23
© Gianni Dagli/CORBIS, 6 (bottom)
© D.Y./Art Resource, NY, 29
© Mary Evans/Edwin Wallace, 10
© Mary Evans Picture Library, 12 (top)
© Werner Forman/CORBIS, 13

© Giraudon/Art Resource, NY, 14
© Historical Picture Archive/CORBIS, 8
© The Image Bank/Getty Images, 4
© Image Select/Art Resource, NY, 20 (top)
© Erich Lessing/Art Resource, NY, 11 (left)
Library of Congress, 18, 20 (bottom), 22
© North Wind Picture Archives, 21
© Photo Disc, 24, 28 (bottom), 30
© The Pierpont Library/Art Resource, NY, 19
© The Schøyen Collection, 6 (top), 11 (inset), 12 (bottom), 15 (both), 17

LIBRARY OF CONGRESS CATALOGING-IN-PUBLICATION DATA

Library of Congress Cataloging-in-Publication Data

Stewart, Gail B., 1949-
  Written communication / by Gail B. Stewart.
    p. cm. — (Yesterday and today)
  Includes bibliographical references and index.
  ISBN 1-56711-834-8 (hardback : alk. paper)
  1. Written communication—History. 2. Writing—History. I. Title. II. Series.

  P211.S687 2004
  302.2'244'09—dc22   2004008390

Table of Contents

The First Written Communication 4

Inventing the Alphabet 6

Beyond Clay Tablets 8

The Basics of Modern Writing 10

The Roots of Printing 12

A Lifetime for a Book 14

Speeding the Printing Process 16

Johannes Gutenberg's Bible 18

The Power of the Printing Press 20

Storing the Written Word: The First Libraries 22

Improving Writing Tools 24

Modernizing Printing 26

Written Communication for the Blind 28

The Computer Age 30

Glossary 32

For More Information 32

Index 32

The First Written Communication

The first written communications were not words, but pictures. Prehistoric people painted on the walls of caves to tell the story of events such as a successful hunt or a frightening storm. When they painted images of charging oxen or dark thunderclouds, they were recording things they had seen. People painted with sticks dipped in charcoal. They also ground certain minerals into a form of paint to add color to the paintings. For example, ocher, or iron ore, was ground to make the colors red and yellow. Some people made brushes by tying bits of animal hair to a stick. Such painting was an easy way to communicate, because everyone could understand the symbols—no matter what language they spoke.

Over the centuries, prehistoric societies changed. Instead of roaming from place to place as hunters, many people settled in villages and became farmers or craftspeople. They needed a way to keep track of the crops they grew or the goods they produced. One way to do this was through picture writing.

Prehistoric people drew pictures on cave walls as the earliest form of written communication.

People drew pictures to represent physical things (above) and then grew to use combinations of drawings, called ideograms (right), to suggest ideas.

Prehistory ——

500 B.C. ——

100 B.C. ——

A.D. 100 ——

200 ——

500 ——

1000 ——

1200 ——

Picture writing was first used around 3500 B.C. by the ancient Sumerians, who lived in what is now the southern part of the Iraq. Sumerian priests used picture writing to keep track of each temple's business. A priest would use a sharp stick to mark on a flat tablet made of soft clay. If a village farmer wished to donate four oxen to the temple, for example, a priest would make a simple picture of an ox's head with four little circles underneath.

Even this new system had its shortcomings, however. It was easy to draw a picture of a physical thing, such as a person or an animal. It was difficult, however, to draw ideas or feelings such as sadness or sickness. To improve written communication, some civilizations began to use ideograms. Ideograms are combinations of pictures that form an idea. For example, a picture of the sun with seven circles underneath it would mean "one week." A picture of an open mouth would mean "to talk." Changing from colorful cave paintings to ideograms, human beings learned how to use writing systems to communicate about a wider variety of things.

1300 ——

1400 ——

1500 ——

1600 ——

1700 ——

1800 ——

1900 ——

2000 ——

2100 ——

Cave Paintings

Some of the oldest examples of picture writing were discovered in caves in France and Spain. It is estimated that these drawings are thirty-seven thousand years old. Cave paintings are not limited to Europe, however. They have been discovered in Africa, Australia, and North and South America, as well.

Inventing the Alphabet

Various cultures gradually streamlined their picture writing. They made the symbols less detailed so they could be drawn quickly. There were still limitations, however. For example, it was impossible to write sentences, or to know when one idea stopped and another began. It was impossible to write people's names, unless their names were also words which could be drawn. Complicated ideas were difficult to write, too—even with ideograms.

Some ancient cultures began to use their symbols in a different way. Instead of having a symbol stand for a word, people used symbols to stand for sounds in their language. With enough symbols—which were called letters—they could write any word or name. A set of letters that stands for the sounds in a language is an alphabet.

The ancient Sumerians are believed to be the first people to develop an alphabet. This occurred between 2800 B.C. and 2400 B.C. Some of the letters were based on the symbols used in ideograms. Eventually, most of the letters used in their

For hundreds of years, people wrote symbols on clay tablets like these. The tablet at the right was a Sumerian count of goats and sheep.

Prehistory

500 B.C.

100 B.C.

A.D. 100

200

500

1000

1200

1300

1400

1500

1600

1700

1800

1900

2000

2100

The English alphabet is similar to the one developed by the Greeks and the Romans.

alphabet barely resembled the original words they once stood for.

Over time, travelers spread the Sumerians' alphabet concept to other cultures. The Indus civilization, which was located in what are now Pakistan and India, and the ancient Egyptians developed their own alphabets. The letters were changed to fit the sounds of each language. Some systems used hundreds of letters, while others needed fewer.

The ancient Greeks developed an alphabet that needed only twenty-four letters. The Romans later used that alphabet, but changed a few letters. The alphabet used today by most Western languages, including English, is based on the Roman alphabet.

As symbols were shortened into simpler letters, it was more difficult for average people to understand them. In many ancient cultures, only specially trained individuals, called scribes, could read and write.

Chinese Characters

The Chinese language does not use an alphabet, but rather a complex system of picture writing. There are more than fifty thousand different symbols, or characters, in written Chinese. To read at a fairly simple level, however, a person must only memorize about two thousand characters.

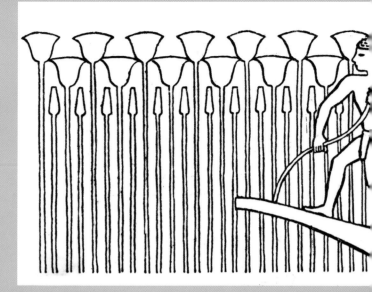

In this drawing (above, right), Egyptians gather reeds along the banks of the Nile River to make papyrus (above), which replaced clay tablets for writing and drawing.

FAST FACT

The word papyrus is the origin of the English word *paper*. To write on papyrus, people used sharp reeds, which they dipped in an ink made of soot, water, and a gum or sap.

Beyond Clay Tablets

The invention of alphabet systems made writing easier. For centuries, scribes wrote down thousands of things—from temple business transactions, histories, and legends to personal letters and collections of poems. For many years, much of the writing in Sumeria and other places in the Middle East was done on clay tablets. Sticks or reeds were used to mark the soft clay. Then the tablet was baked in the sun, and the writing was preserved.

The ancient Egyptians found a material far easier to write on. Called papyrus, it was made from the reeds that grew near the banks of the Nile River. After overlapping thin strips from the inside stems into flat sheets, the Egyptians would hammer them flat. Then the flattened sheets were dried in the sun. Papyrus was far less bulky than clay

Prehistory

500 B.C.

100 B.C.

A.D. 100

200

500

1000

1200

1300

1400

1500

1600

1700

1800

1900

2000

2100

tablets. A single sheet of papyrus was enough to write a letter or a short list. For longer jobs, the Egyptians used sap to glue several sheets of papyrus together and rolled them into a scroll.

The Egyptians sold the papyrus they made to neighboring people, such as the Greeks and Romans. While the papyrus reed was plentiful along the Nile River, however, the demand for it became very high. By about 500 B.C., papyrus had become very scarce. As a result, a new writing material became desirable—parchment.

Parchment was made from the skins of sheep, calves, and goats. It was made by soaking and stretching a skin on a special wooden frame for ten days, then allowing it to dry in the sun. The skin would then be scraped with a sharp knife until it was smooth and clean. Parchment became the most commonly used writing material throughout most of the world until the Middle Ages, the time between the fifth century A.D. and A.D. 1500. Parchment had an advantage over papyrus. While papyrus tended to crack and decay over the years, parchment was a far more durable material.

Scribes

Ancient civilizations, such as the Egyptians and Sumerians, depended on scribes, or professional writers. Scribes, who were always male, were trained at special schools. Since scribes were the only people who could read and write in those times, they were respected as important members of society.

The Basics of Modern Writing

While most of the world was using parchment, the Chinese had developed an even better writing surface—paper. In A.D. 105, an emperor's adviser named Ts'ai Lun noticed that wasps built their nests from bark and water. He believed that the substance created by the wasps would be a good writing surface, so he gathered bark from a mulberry tree and hammered it into a pulp. After straining dirt and other impurities from the pulp, he let it dry in the sun. The emperor was so pleased with the invention that he made Ts'ai Lun a nobleman.

Ts'ai Lun, an adviser to China's emperor, hammered tree bark into pulp and then let it dry in the sun to create paper.

Prehistory

500 B.C.

100 B.C.

A.D. 100

200

500

1000

1200

1300

1400

1500

1600

1700

1800

1900

2000

2100

The Chinese used dyes to make colorful paper (above), a technique that later influenced European printing (left).

Chinese papermakers found that substances other than tree bark could also be made into paper. By pounding rope, rags, silk, and even old fishing nets, they could create paper that was cheap and easy to use. They also experimented with dyes to create colorful paper.

The Chinese kept their paper a secret for more than six hundred years. During a war against Arabs in the seventh century, Chinese prisoners revealed the art of creating paper. After that, people throughout the Middle East began to make paper. They, too, kept the process a secret for about four hundred years. In 1150, Arabs in Spain and Italy built paper mills there. After that, other European countries began to produce paper, too.

The Chinese developed block printing in 618 to quickly print pictures of Buddha (right). About 250 years later they used block printing to publish scrolls like this one (below).

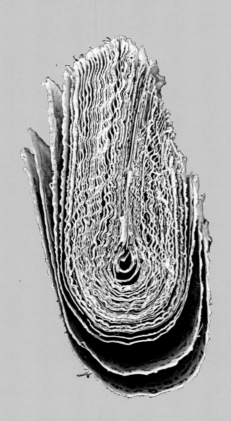

The Roots of Printing

Though the invention of paper had provided people with an excellent writing material, written communication was still a time-consuming activity. Individual manuscripts, or writings, could only be done by hand, one at a time.

The solution to this problem was discovered in China, about five hundred years after Ts'ai Lun invented paper. Historians say that Buddhism, a religion practiced by many Chinese people, had a key role in this discovery. Buddhists followed the teachings of a priest named Siddhartha Gautama, whom they called the Buddha. To show their devotion to the Buddha, his followers displayed statues and paintings of him in their homes and temples.

Drawing individual portraits of the Buddha was time-consuming. In A.D. 618, priests carved a wooden block with the Buddha's image and coated the block with ink. They pressed the ink to a piece of paper and found that the image had been transferred to the paper. Enthusiastic about the results, they printed thousands of pictures of the Buddha for his followers.

Cloth makers had used blocks for many years to decorate fabrics, but block printing had never been used to communicate an image or message. It was not long before priests began combining the picture with some of the sayings of the Buddha.

Using block printing, priests created the first printed book in A.D. 868. Called *The Diamond Sutra*, the book was a collection of the Buddha's sermons. It was made from seven long sheets of paper that were glued together and rolled onto a scroll. Other Chinese priests were impressed with the work, and many had wooden blocks carved to create their own books. Written communication had taken a big leap forward, for printing made it easy to circulate information to large numbers of people.

The publication of The Diamond Sutra, *a collection of Buddha's sermons, caused more books to be made with block printing.*

FAST FACT

The man who printed *The Diamond Sutra* put a special page in the book, dedicating it to the memory of his parents. He also insisted that the book be distributed free to anyone who wanted to read it.

Prehistory ——

500 B.C. ——

100 B.C. ——

A.D. 100 ——

200 ——

500 ——

1000 ——

1200 ——

1300 ——

1400 ——

1500 ——

1600 ——

1700 ——

1800 ——

1900 ——

2000 ——

2100 ——

A Lifetime for a Book

Although the Chinese were using block printing by A.D. 868, people throughout the rest of the world knew nothing about it. Travel between Europe and China was almost nonexistent. As a result, the Chinese system of printing was limited to China for centuries.

During the Middle Ages in Europe, which was the period from roughly the fifth century A.D. to A.D. 1500, books were written by hand. As in China, books being made in Europe were almost all religious texts, from copies of the Bible to prayer books. Monks or priests spent years creating copies of important books. They were done in neat, careful script and contained colorful drawings and designs. Such books were known as illuminated manuscripts, because the jewel-like colors decorating the books seemed to glow. In fact, some of the colors were created by crushing jewels into the ink. Monks made the paper sparkle by highlighting some pages in gold or silver.

It was not uncommon for a monk to work twenty or thirty years to finish a long manuscript. Some monks actually worked their entire lives on one book. The monks took special care to make the writing neat and fancy. For example, a capital letter at the beginning of a chapter was almost always oversized, with miniature designs of animals or flowers.

During the Middle Ages, monks worked in special writing rooms and copied books by hand, sometimes for their entire lives.

Monks took special care to make their writing very neat and fancy, and they often decorated the books with colorful drawings and designs.

The writing was done in a special room called a scriptorium. Though some rooms in a monastery had a fireplace, the scriptorium did not. After all, a fire could wipe out lifetimes of manuscripts—so monks worked in the cold during the winter months. Since no lanterns or candles were permitted, manuscript writing was only done during the daylight hours.

The books themselves were very valuable when they were complete. Many were kept in the monasteries, while others were sold to wealthy nobles who could afford them. Owning a book in those days was something only the rich could enjoy.

Prehistory ——

500 B.C. ——

100 B.C. ——

A.D. 100 ——

200 ——

500 ——

1000 ——

1200 ——

1300 ——

1400 ——

1500 ——

1600 ——

1700 ——

1800 ——

1900 ——

2000 ——

2100 ——

Pi Sheng made individual words out of clay tiles and then moved them around a metal tray to form different sentences. This allowed him to print books quickly.

Speeding the Printing Process

A third breakthrough in written communication occurred in China in 1041. A printer named Pi Sheng had been looking for ways to print books more quickly. He decided to cut the printing blocks to separate the individual words from each other. That way, the blocks, or type, could be reused to form different sentences in new books. This technique was called movable type.

If this new process were to work, Pi Sheng knew he had to find a stronger material than wood. Though easy to carve, wooden type would wear out quickly if used over and over. Instead, Pi Sheng made tiles from clay. He then baked the type, which made the tiles hard and durable. Pi Sheng encountered another important problem with the new type, too—how to keep the individual clay tiles from moving during printing. He solved this problem by making a tray out of metal, which was the exact size of a page to be printed. The ink was spread over the tray of tiles, and then paper was pressed against it.

There was an important problem that Pi Sheng could not solve, however. Since the Chinese use picture symbols rather than an alphabet, Chinese printers would need a different tile for every word. That amounted to many thousands of tiles.

The movable type system was tried in another Asian civilization—Korea. Korea did not have hardwood trees, so its printers were limited to soft woods, such as pine. Because block printing did not work well with soft woods, Korean printers began to experiment with metal type. They heated metal until it was a thick liquid and poured it into little molds to make type. The metal type was even more durable than the clay tiles Pi Sheng had made. Even so, the Korean written language was based on the Chinese model, so movable-type printing was not developed there, either. The system of movable type, which would revolutionize printing everywhere else in the world, was not thought of again for four hundred years.

Korean printers adopted the Chinese system, but they used metal type instead of clay tiles to print the Korean alphabet.

Prehistory

500 B.C.

100 B.C.

A.D. 100

200

500

1000

1200

1300

1400

1500

1600

1700

1800

1900

2000

2100

17

Johannes Gutenberg's Bible

During the time that Chinese printers had developed and abandoned the idea of movable type, Europeans were still making books by hand. In the 1300s, the Italian explorer Marco Polo wrote about his journey to China and described block printing done there. He told about the Chinese paper money and playing cards that had been printed with carved blocks, and the idea caught on in Europe.

Although simple things such as playing cards and pictures could be easily printed with wooden blocks, books were a different matter. As Pi Sheng had learned in China centuries before, wooden blocks took a very long time to carve. Printing books by that method would waste time, rather than save it.

Gutenberg (right) invented a movable-type printing press that could print ten large sheets of paper in an hour.

Prehistory ——

500 B.C. ——

100 B.C. ——

A.D. 100 ——

200 ——

500 ——

1000 ——

1200 ——

1300 ——

1400 ——

1500 ——

1600 ——

1700 ——

1800 ——

1900 ——

2000 ——

2100 ——

The first book Gutenberg printed was a 1,280-page Bible. More books could be printed because of the new machine's speed.

In the mid-1400s, a German printer named Johannes Gutenberg began to experiment with movable lead type. Historians say that Gutenberg had no way of knowing about the movable Chinese tiles or the movable Korean metal type. Instead, he thought of the idea himself as he looked for a better, faster way of printing.

For a printing press, Gutenberg adapted a machine that had been used for years to press cheeses and grapes. The press was a large wooden frame. On one section of the frame, Gutenberg added a table on which the tray of type could be arranged. The other section was a large wooden block that could press the paper against the type. Gutenberg first arranged the metal letters of type to form blocks of sentences, or paragraphs. He spread ink over the type by hand, using soft leather balls filled with wool. Then, after placing a sheet of paper on the type, he turned a wooden screw that lowered the block onto the paper. The pressure transferred the ink to the paper.

The first book Gutenberg printed was the Bible. It was a great challenge, since each book was 1,280 pages long. It took him five years to print 210 copies—180 on paper and 30 on parchment made from calfskin. The printing was completed in 1456. It required six individual printing presses as well as a number of printer's assistants to complete.

Within a few years, printing shops had sprung up throughout Europe, building on Gutenberg's ideas. By 1470, more than four thousand books a year were being printed. By 1500, there were more than fifteen hundred print shops in Europe, and they had printed more than 1 million books.

FAST FACT

Using his movable-type press, Gutenberg could print ten large sheets of paper each hour—a task that would have taken a monk more than a month to do by hand.

The Power of the Printing Press

The development of the printing press caused several changes in society. One was a demand among common people for books on a variety of subjects—not just religious texts. While Gutenberg's Bible, like earlier handwritten manuscripts, had been in Latin, people wanted books that were printed in everyday language they could understand. In England, for example, fifteenth-century printers turned out copies of favorite legends, such as *King Arthur* and Chaucer's *Canterbury Tales*.

The printing press also resulted in the birth of newspapers. The earliest newspapers were printed in

After Gutenberg invented the printing press (right), people began to demand books they could read in their own language (above).

The First American Newspaper

The first newspaper published in the American colonies was called *Public Occurrences Both Foreign and Domestic*. Its first issue was critical of the British governor of Massachusetts. As a result, it was forced to go out of business.

the early 1600s in Germany. They were usually one-page weeklies that reported recent events in politics, business, and the arts. Soon newspapers were being printed in other countries, too.

In the American colonies, the printing press served an important function. The first print shop in America was set up in Cambridge, Massachusetts, by Stephen Daye and his son Matthew in 1639. By 1690, there was a newspaper in Boston, followed by others in all the major cities in the colonies. The newspapers helped inform the colonists of new taxes and laws the British imposed on them. Such reporting often angered the British governors. They ordered some newspapers to stop printing stories about such topics.

The leaders of the American Revolution understood how important the press was in keeping people informed and educated. In fact, the First Amendment to the Constitution guaranteed freedom of the press. Even though an article might be controversial or critical of the government, the newspaper would be allowed to print it.

Benjamin Franklin used his newspaper, the Philadelphia Gazette, *to inform Americans about the American Revolution.*

An American Printer

Benjamin Franklin, one of the most important figures in the American Revolution, prided himself on being a printer. His newspaper was the *Philadelphia Gazette.* Though Franklin lived about three hundred years after Gutenberg's time, Franklin's press looked remarkably like the one used to print the Gutenberg Bible.

Prehistory

500 B.C.

100 B.C.

A.D. 100

200

500

1000

1200

1300

1400

1500

1600

1700

1800

1900

2000

2100

Storing the Written Word: The First Libraries

Benjamin Franklin helped create the first circulating library in the colonies.

Since ancient times, people have saved some of their written communication. Archaeologists, those who study long-ago cultures, have found collections of ancient records on clay tablets, papyrus scrolls, and parchment. Many of the early libraries consisted of religious or government writings and were owned by priests or wealthy rulers. Even after printing became common, libraries were usually owned by universities. Individual readers could look at books in the library, but rarely were they permitted to borrow them.

It was much the same in the American colonies. Some of the wealthier people might own a title or two, but rarely more than that. In 1731, Benjamin Franklin, then a printer in Philadelphia, proposed that people combine their books, and then all would have access to the entire library. In addition, he suggested that people who did not own books could pay a small yearly fee, and this would entitle them to use the library. This was the first circulating library in the American colonies.

At first, about fifty people contributed books. They were mostly nonfiction, on subjects such as mythology, astronomy, and

Prehistory —

500 B.C. —

100 B.C. —

A.D. 100 —

200 —

500 —

1000 —

1200 —

1300 —

1400 —

1500 —

1600 —

1700 —

1800 —

1900 —

2000 —

2100 —

world history. One family contributed a large dictionary. The library grew quickly, for as people subscribed, the library could afford to buy new titles. Franklin and his friends took turns keeping the library at their homes. Within a year, the library was declared a success, and other cities throughout the colonies created libraries of their own. The more people used the libraries, the more informed they became about important subjects.

The Library of Congress in Washington, D.C., was established in 1800 and is the world's largest library.

The Library of Alexandria

One of the most extraordinary libraries of the ancient world was in Alexandria, Egypt. It contained more than four hundred thousand scrolls containing information on history, literature, mathematics, and science. Legends say that the library was burned by invading Roman troops, and no sign of it or its contents has ever been found.

Improving Writing Tools

The printing press was responsible for great strides in written communication. There were also important developments in writing tools used by individuals. Through the 1700s, the most commonly used writing tool was the quill pen. It was usually made from the feather of a swan or goose. The tip was cut with a sharp knife to make a point, called a nib. When the nib was dipped in ink, the quill pen was ready to use. The quill had to be inked frequently.

Beginning in the eighteenth century, people began to make pens out of metal. Called fountain pens, they were far more durable than quill pens, and they were filled with ink with an eye dropper. They did not have to be dipped in ink like quill pens. Over the years, pen makers improved the filling system so that cartridges filled with ink could be slipped into the barrel of the pen. In 1938, the Biro brothers from Hungary developed a pen that used a rotating ball to apply the ink to paper. Known as ballpoint pens, or Biros, they were far cheaper and easier to use than fountain pens.

The pencil, first used in England in the late eighteenth century, gave people an alternative to ink pens. It consisted of a stick of dry, black marking material in a

Quill pens, which had to be dipped into ink, were replaced in the eighteenth century with pens made of metal and filled with ink.

their fingers. This way, they did not give away their position in the field by using light. Barbier's code system was impractical for anything but brief messages, since the various placement of dots stood for words, rather than letters of the alphabet.

Braille experimented with various formations of dots and settled on a six-dot system. By using a maximum of six dots per letter, he could write any word and still have symbols for punctuation and commonly used words such as *the* and *with*. The raised-dot alphabet was called braille, after its inventor. It continues to be the most important method of written communication used by blind people all over the world.

FAST FACT

Not only can blind people read braille, but by using special machines, they can write messages in braille. The machine, called a braillewriter, has six keys and can print any combination of the sixty-three braille symbols.

Blind people all over the world use braille both to read and to write messages.

Prehistory ——

500 B.C. ——

100 B.C. ——

A.D. 100 ——

200 ——

500 ——

1000 ——

1200 ——

1300 ——

1400 ——

1500 ——

1600 ——

1700 ——

1800 ——

1900 ——

2000 ——

2100 ——

The invention of computers led to increased speed in the production and circulation of written information.

The Computer Age

Although many advances have made written communication faster, none has been more important than the invention of the computer. In the mid-1960s, printing shops began to use computers to regulate a number of jobs. They managed the amount and color of ink to be used, the placement of photographs in the document, and the placement and folding of paper.

Computers have created more possibilities for personal printing, too. Using a personal computer, a person can create newspapers, reports, or books. Once the design and layout of the document is satisfactory, the information is transferred to a disk and sent to a printer.

In addition to changing the way printing is done, computers have added a new dimension in written communication. In 1969, U.S. military officials designed a system that allowed computers at various military bases to share important information. This system was expanded over the years and developed into the Internet, a network of computers around the world.

On the Internet, users can find information from tens of thousands of sources. People can send and receive messages instantly using the computer, too. Called electronic mail, or e-mail, these messages allow people thousands of miles apart to hold conversations using their computers. E-mail is the fastest-growing form of personal written communication. In fact, in 2000 it was estimated that the average computer user received more than fifty e-mails per week.

Written communication has changed a great deal since ancient civilizations kept records on clay tablets. From the invention of alphabets to the development of newer and more powerful printing systems, people have always worked hard to find quicker and more accurate ways to communicate with one another.

FACT:

Many companies that have tapped into computer networks send advertisements in the form of e-mails. Unwanted advertisements are known as spam.

E-mail allows people to instantly send written messages to people thousands of miles away.

Prehistory ——

500 B.C. ——

100 B.C. ——

A.D. 100 ——

200 ——

500 ——

1000 ——

1200 ——

1300 ——

1400 ——

1500 ——

1600 ——

1700 ——

1800 ——

1900 ——

2000 ——

2100 ——

Glossary

alphabet: A set of letters used to represent sounds.

braille: A reading and writing system used by blind people.

block printing: The earliest method of printing, in which each page of print was carved on a wooden block.

compositor: In earlier print shops, the worker who would set type by hand.

e-mail: Electronic mail that travels instantly along computer networks.

graphite: A form of carbon used in pencils.

ideogram: A system of combining pictures to represent ideas. Ancient people used ideograms to communicate ideas that were hard to draw pictures of, such as lengths of time.

illuminated manuscript: Usually a religious document that has been written by hand and decorated with bright colors and pictures.

linotype: A machine invented in 1886 that allowed type to be set mechanically, rather than by hand.

nib: The sharp point of a pen.

papyrus: A paperlike substance made by ancient Egyptians from a reed found near the Nile River.

parchment: Thick writing material made from the skins of calves or goats.

quill pens: Early pens made of the feathers of birds.

scribe: A professional writer in ancient times.

scriptorium: The room in a monastery during the Middle Ages where monks worked on their illuminated manuscripts.

scroll: Several sheets of paper glued together and rolled onto a stick. Early books were put on scrolls.

For More Information

Books

Leonard Everett Fisher, *Colonial Craftsmen: The Printers.* New York: Marshall Cavendish, 2000.

Russell Freedman, *Out of Darkness: The Story of Louis Braille.* New York: Clarion Press, 1997.

Anita Ganeri, *The Story of Writing and Printing.* New York: Oxford University Press, 1995.

Geography Department of Runestone Press, *Scrawl! Writing in Ancient Times.* Minneapolis: Runestone Press, 1994.

Lois Warburton, *The Beginning of Writing.* San Diego: Lucent Books, 1990.

Internet Sources

The British Museum, "Ancient Egypt," 1999. www.ancientegypt.co.uk. Excellent, colorful photographs of ancient hieroglyphics and the story of how such writing has been translated.

Dot Print, "Printing World: An Industry Born," www.dotprint.com. Excellent details on the printing industry, with a time line of important printing events since Gutenberg's Bible.

Index

Alexandria, Egypt, 23
alphabet, 6–7, 8, 16
American Revolution, 21

Bible, 18–19
blind people, 28–29
block printing, 12, 13, 14, 17, 18
books, 13, 14–15, 16, 18–19, 20
Braille, Louis, 28–29
Buddha, 12–13

cave paintings, 4, 5
China, 7, 10, 12–13, 16
clay tablets, 8, 22
computers, 30–31

Diamond Sutra, The, 13

e-mail, 31

Franklin, Benjamin, 21, 22

Gutenburg, Johannes, 18–19, 26

ideograms, 4, 5, 6
illuminated manuscripts, 14
Internet, 31

König, Friedrich, 26
Korea, 16, 17

letters, 6

libraries, 22–23
linotype, 26, 27

Mergenthaler, Ottmar, 26-27
metal type, 16, 17, 18, 19
Middle Ages, 9, 14–15
monks, 14–15, 19
movable type, 16–17, 18, 19

newspaper, 20–21, 27

paper, 10–11, 12
papyrus, 8–9, 22
parchment, 9, 10, 22
pencils, 24-15
pens, 24
Pi Sheng, 16–17, 18

picture writing, 4–5, 7
Polo, Marco, 18
printing, 12–13, 26-27
printing press, 20–21, 24, 26–27

scribes, 7, 8, 9, 14
scriptorium, 15
Sumeria, 5, 6–7, 8, 9
symbols, 6

Ts'ai Lun, 10, 12
typesetting, 26–27
typewriter, 25

wood blocks, 12, 13, 18
writing tools, 24–25